The Black Person's Guide To Adult Education And Economic Empowerment

by
LeDene Lewis

AFRICAN AMERICAN IMAGES
1992
CHICAGO, ILLINOIS

Cover illustration by Reginald Mackey

Photo credits: William Hall

First edition, first printing

© Copyright 1992 by LeDene Lewis

DEDICATION

*I dedicate this book to my husband
Ray, daughters Jessica and Walonda,
my mother Florence, my brother James, my
in-laws, and to you, dear reader, for having
the courage to step out of your comfort zone
to further your education and become
educationally empowered.
I bid you Godspeed.*

CONTENTS

INTRODUCTION

On behalf of your African American family, particularly those pioneering Blacks who gave their lives so that you could become educated and employed, I sincerely thank you for making the decision to return to the classroom and job market. Thank you for refusing to continue to allow your brain to feed solely on trite TV programming or other distractions that are neither educationally sound nor productive. Congratulations for clearing the hurdles of "put-downs" and "you-can't-do-its" that you may have heard from "friends" as you talked about going back to school. Thank you for starting a journey that will eventually launch you into the career God intended.

You might be thinking, "Wow! Do I deserve all of THAT?" Oh, yes. When you signed on the line to receive a seat in a classroom, you made many statements:

◆ I am NOT going to end up as just another negative statistic about African Americans.

◆ I WILL be a productive member of society by preparing myself to earn my own way.

◆ I have FAITH in my ability to succeed despite the obstacles.

◆ I know that I am a ROLE MODEL for those younger eyes that are watching me and whose bodies will do as I do. I want them to see me succeed so that they will want to try too.

◆ I am NOT a failure because failing is not trying; and I at least took this step.

How I wish I could tell you that the hard part is over.

I wish I could tell you that now that you're registered for your courses or about to be, that it will be all A's, awards, and cake from here. It will not. In fact, don't allow any school's admissions personnel to give you that impression. Education is the forerunner for employment; therefore, the experience should be treated as if it WERE employment. This means a certain amount of work is required at this point.

The truth of the matter is that you are only about 20 percent over the hard part. Registration is a big, big step; however, as an instructor and former business school administrator, I can tell you with certainty that there are several trackblocking hurdles coming that you will have to clear in order to reach that prized cap and gown and "new-job paycheck". These hurdles were analyzed by a team of educators who compiled a study listing over 1,000 reasons why adults drop out of school.

This book was written so that you will know ahead of time what those hurdles are and how to clear them so that you can remain on the path that leads to education and empowerment. The most common education stoppers for adult students are:

◆ Family/Friends
◆ Transportation
◆ Financial Concerns
◆ Child Care
◆ Professional Attire
◆ Health/Nutrition
◆ Attendance

Of course, no book can resolve every problem you might encounter during the length of your training. However, here are some guidelines that have proven to be useful and will work for you if you are determined enough to apply them and committed enough to STAY IN SCHOOL — no matter what! Let's begin by laying a solid foundation.

PUTTING FIRST THINGS FIRST

If education is high on your list of things that are important to you (and it should be), you will find yourself making a way for it — no matter what it takes. You should know that other things WILL compete for your time. Whenever you make a move towards the positive, the negative will attempt to crowd, discourage, or defeat you. This is not superstitious "mumbo jumbo," it's just how life is. In order to be successful and complete any retraining program, you MUST:

◆ **Realize that you are not just going to school.** Actually, you are:

◆ thanking those who gave their lives so you could go to school;

◆ telling those young eyes watching you that Black is not a word that stands for ignorance — despite what they see or hear on TV;

◆ making a statement to yourself and others that yours is not a wasted life.

You've got to understand that whatever you do, whether it is sitting and wasting away or recharging your brain cells in a classroom, your actions influence the lives of others. If you will remember that, you may not be so quick to quit the moment you feel particularly challenged in your studies. Try to see your training time as an **investment** in yourself, your family, and your nation.

♦ **Know that classrooms offer much more than piles of homework.** You get:

♦ a chance to be around others who have also made a life-changing decision. Positive friendships can develop. You'll need new friends if your current comrades desert you;

♦ a chance to measure yourself against standards that are higher than what you accepted before you started school.

♦ **Know that you will give your time and money to whatever you consider to be valuable.** See your future, YOURSELF as valuable. It really is okay to put yourself way up there on your own priority list as long as you know that what you want is good for you and others.

As you are reading this book, do yourself a favor: Ask yourself how each hurdle and solution pertains to your own situation. You will be glad you took the extra time to digest what you are reading. Complete the exercises. Psychologists (and lawyers) agree that writing something down endears (or commits) a person to what was written. Take the time to complete each exercise as HONESTLY as possible. Respond as if no one except you and God will see what you've written.

Just one more word before we begin. If you are on general assistance and are struggling with the notion that welfare pays better than employment, you just may be tempted to believe that the effort it takes to educate yourself is an unnecessary hardship. Let's reason together.

There are many ways a person can receive "pay". Welfare checks and even paychecks from jobs are but one way. They both are money. But there are other "payoffs" education and work offer that welfare doesn't. And they are things that are very difficult to place a dollar value on. For instance, let's say you owned a department store in which I could buy some items for my spirit and soul. How much would you charge for self-esteem? How much would you charge for self-respect? How much for an opportunity to move towards the positive and change lifestyles? **Don't be fooled. Getting something for nothing does not "pay"; IT ROBS.**

It robs you of your dignity and, due to non-use, corrodes that precious brain you were given. Telling yourself that it is okay to want to spend the rest of your life on just enough money and so-called benefits to get by is the same as giving yourself permission to paralyze your potential. **Ignore the voice of where you are or have been; listen and stay tuned in to the voice of where you're headed.**

Thanks again for trying education — and CONGRATULATIONS!

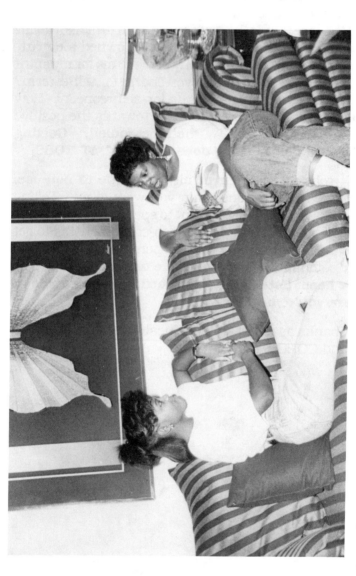

Making those close to you a vital part of your accomplishments is a sure-fire way to gain their support.

FAMILY AND FRIENDS

As you make your move to get ahead in life, those closest to you may bid for your attention to the point of distracting you from your goals. Are they being unreasonable? Not really. They are just being human.

Gloria's Story

"I'll have to drop out, Ms. Lewis. I don't know why this is, but all of a sudden, my husband won't give me a moment's peace. I try to sneak off to do my homework, and he tracks me down and picks at me about stupid stuff—things that never bothered him before. Well it all came to a head last night," complained Gloria.

"I knew I had a business math midterm exam today, and that I needed to practice doing story problems. So I told Jake — that's my husband —that I was going to the basement to fold clothes. See, I knew that if he thought I was doing housework, he'd leave me alone for awhile. Well I guess I was too long foldin' clothes because he came down to see what was taking me so long.

He caught me doing schoolwork and accused me of putting school ahead of him and the family. He said I was doing homework when I should have been doing HOUSE WORK! Does that make sense to you? I'm telling you, the man's elevator does not go all the way up the shaft, if you know what I mean. I have to drop out just to keep peace," she said.

I talked with Gloria a bit longer and discovered that the "before" she referred to when she said that small things never bothered Jake meant before she signed up for school.

PROBLEM: Someone close to you gets upset whenever you even talk about school. The chief complaint is that you spend too much time away from him or her.

SOLUTION: That person may be convinced that once you graduate, you won't love him or her anymore. Or, perhaps it is believed that you will meet someone else in one of your classes whom you'll be attracted to. What to do? Search yourself to see if the person complaining has a valid reason. Look at it this way: Am I being loving towards you if every time you come around, I behave as if I couldn't be bothered because, after all, I AM a student now, and, well, you'll just have to understand? Do you know what YOU'D start to think? You'd think that I didn't love you. You would probably start to complain every time you felt I took too much time away from you in order to study. The last thing you would want me to talk about would be anything that had to do with your going to school.

Has someone made "you're-neglecting-me" noises to you? When was the last time that person got your undivided attention? No TV, no kids, no company, just you two? If it is a kid who is complaining, can you plan time alone with him or her? The point is that you have to take time for your loved ones. If your studying becomes such a source of irritation that your peace is routinely upset, **you don't have to quit school; even if the loved one threatens to leave you if you stay in.**

Instead you could:

- ◆ Draw the complainer to you by allowing him or her to help you with your homework.

- ◆ Be certain to **share the joy** of every sign of success, such as an "A" on a report card or paper. Better yet, find a way to make the other person feel that his or her help contributed greatly to your success. "If you hadn't helped me with the research, I might never have finished that report!" is music to the ears of one who needs to feel needed and useful.

- ◆ Find more agreeable times to study. For example, consider studying at school after classes, before you go home. Or study early in the morning while your household still sleeps. How about using half of your lunch hour for studying at work? Can you get to school early — before your classes start? You could study then.

- ◆ Never pester your loved ones about their NOT going to school. Encourage, yes. Nag, criticize or belittle, no. You're working on loving them, remember?

A HAPPY ENDING: "Guess what!" Gloria said rushing into my office. "For the past couple of weeks, I've made it a point to ask Jake to double check my work — he's always been a whiz at math, y'know. Anyway, guess what he's been doing! Instead of criticizing me about doing homework, he now tells me I HAVE to study! Isn't that a kick? I guess I won't have to quit after all!"

MAKING THOSE CLOSE TO YOU A VITAL PART OF YOUR ACCOMPLISHMENTS IS A SURE-FIRE WAY TO GAIN THEIR SUPPORT.

3

List ways whereby you can get ample study time in and yet not neglect your loved ones:

1) _____

2) _____

3) _____

4) _____

Isaiah's Story

"Yo, yo, Mzz Lewis, see I was goin' to study to make up all them tests and assignments, y'understand? But, check this, like, my old lady don't cruise so good cuz her heart is bad and like she really needs me to kick some food into her kitch and other stuff, y'understand?" complained Isaiah.

Yes, I understood. I understood that Isaiah had missed approximately 30 percent of his training so far due to family "emergencies." I understood that with three brothers, two sisters, and a sickly mom all pulling on this father stand-in, Isaiah was in danger of being another drop-out statistic. He had plenty of drive, determination, and personal appeal. He was badly in need of more home support.

"...so like, that's why I got all them makeups to do, but check this: I'll stay up all night and make up the work, and I'll kick all those tests after school tomorrow if you just don't kick me out. Word!" he tried to assure me.

Isaiah and I eventually came to an agreement about how the assignments and tests could be made up; but after he left my office, I felt sharp pangs of guilt because I was yes-ing a situation I knew most bosses wouldn't tolerate for an instant.

Schoolwork is preparation for employment. I knew that if Isaiah's family continues to pull on him after he's employed, he won't STAY employed. Or he would never be promoted. His mother may scream racial prejudice when her son gets fired, but the truth of the matter is that Isaiah could potentially be fired for not being on the company's premises long enough to satisfactorily perform the job. How was I preparing him for employment by constantly allowing him to make up his work on HIS schedule? Will his bosses be charmed by his well-meaning intentions? Or will they more likely be impressed by his showing up for work every day and not having to routinely leave early? My heart knew the answer.

If Isaiah could just get his family to realize that he was not just going to school, and if he hasn't isolated them by shutting them out of his school experience, his mom may be more willing to call on someone else for her needs.

PROBLEM: Your family is dependent upon you to do shopping, household chores, errands, babysitting,

5

etc., and you start to feel too bogged down to continue your training.

SOLUTION: If you have not isolated your family, and have instead made them to feel that you NEED them in order to succeed (because you really do), they may be more willing to explore other ways to get chores, etc., done. You must ask them. Don't demand — just ask. Make them aware that there is a lot at stake.

Also, try some old-fashioned bargaining: If I can have just two hours of undisturbed study time, I'll shop for what you need tomorrow...I'll read you a bedtime story two nights in a row... I'll (now you fill in the blanks):

1)_____

2)_____

3)_____

4)_____

BARGAIN FOR STUDY TIME.
STICK WITH THE BARGAIN.

Lilly's Story

It took what seemed forever to encourage Lilly to look at me. She was a dear, almost fragile woman and a model student. She had signed up for one of our most intense secretarial programs and, despite verbal abuse from home, had maintained a straight A average through six out of six card markings. With only two more semesters to go until graduation, she now sat before me with a plea to allow her to drop out of school. Her reasons were weak, and she knew it.

"I know all this seems silly, but...well...I'm starting to believe that school is not for me," said Lilly.

"But you have all A's," I protested.

She looked up and smiled for the first time since coming into my office, "Yes, I know."

"And you tutor your classmates," I continued.

"Well I never said that I wasn't grasping the material..." she defended.

"Well what is it then? I mean REALLY?" I tried to discover.

Silence.

I switched tactics. "Lilly, does your father still support you?" Her father springs for the tuition each month. It's a loan just until she can get back on her feet. She had gone through a messy divorce from an abusive alcoholic and was temporarily living with her folks. My thinking was that maybe he had changed his mind about paying.

"Oh, yes!" she rose and paced. "He supports me all right!" The heat of her response surprised me a little. "And I had better make it too, boy!" She plopped back down. "I'll NEVER hear the end of it if I don't!" Her eyes and wry smile told me her dad was riding her a little too hard again.

"Do YOU think you won't make it?" I asked softly.

"Oh, Mrs. Lewis! What if I don't! What if everything he's been telling me is really TRUE! What if I'm not a 'learner'—like he says I'm not?" she pleaded.

"Are you sure that's what he's saying? Maybe he didn't mean..." I inquired.

She popped up again, arms waving. "He's ALWAYS saying that! Both he and my mother. The only reason he agreed to give me the loan is so that he could hold it over me if I fail!" Lilly answered.

"But..." I countered gently, "you're NOT failing."

Lilly stopped pacing.

"So...maybe...they are not right about you in this particular area?" I suggested.

She reseated herself and faced me squarely. All of the anger and anxiousness were gone. "Well now," she said firmly, "maybe they're not."

8

Lilly wanted to drop out so she could get the "see-I-told-you-so's" from her father over and done. Despite concrete evidence to the contrary, she believed she was a failure because her parents had programmed her with a lifetime flow of negative language.

PROBLEM: A family member whose opinions you value says that you'll never make it and that you are wasting your time by trying. You're told that since you've never finished anything you've started in your life, you probably won't finish your training either, and on and on and on.

SOLUTION: You will very quickly discover that your teachers and anyone else directly tied to your professional development will be working with a different side of you than your sideline critics see. Your teachers will be working with the you that took that all-important first step by signing up for classes. As you begin to respond to the guidance you receive in school, you'll naturally begin to build up your own faith in your ability to succeed and you'll start to feel more confident. The more confident you are, the more you succeed and the more you'll believe. Soon you will hear fewer negative comments from your critics because they will begin to see and respond to the you that your supporters see.

Lilly needed a booster shot in her self-esteem. **She needed** to listen more to the people who believed in her and less to her **negative critics.**

How is YOUR self-esteem? List some people that you will be able to turn to in case you need an esteem booster:

1)_____ 2)_____

YOU WILL FIND THE MOST EFFECTIVE SELF-ESTEEM BOOSTER LOOKING BACK AT YOU IN THE MIRROR.

Bernadette's Story

"See, Ms. Lewis, I used to hang with the Sisters We..." Bernadette explained.

"Sisters...We?" I asked.

"Uh, yeah. Just the girlfriends, y'know. Hangin' and bein' one. I met them at Station Place," she continued. Station Place was a local night-club.

"So...am I to understand that you want to drop out of school because of a... women's... club?" I inquired with disbelief.

"Well, see, it's not exactly a club. It's more like...a support group, y'know what I'm saying?" she tried to convince me.

"A support group," I said flatly. "At a bar."

"Uh, yeah. Anyway... it's just that... well, I don't seem to fit in anymore since I started here. And it's not just with the Sisters We that I don't fit in. It's with everyone at the Station. They all say I've changed too much," she complained.

"How do they say you've changed?" I probed.

"They say that I think that I'm... SOME-

THING... now that I'm going to school..." Bernadette exclaimed.

Although my heart went out to Bernadette, there was no way I was going to give her up to the Station without a fight.

PROBLEM: Your friends put you down because you go to or are thinking about going to school.

SOLUTION: Look up the definition of the word friend. I found definitions that described friend as a supportive person who was not hostile, but who, instead, showed affection or warm personal regard toward another person. Now, let me ask you. Is a person showing you support, affection, or warm personal regard by telling you that by investing time in yourself (and not in them) you are WASTING your time? Sounds like hostility to me — not friendship. Friendship says, "School? You? Go on, girlfriend!" Or, "Hey, Homey! YOU'RE taking up computers?? Well, kick it then! That's all right!" Or, "Listen, I'll watch your kid for you while you study." Friendship DOES NOT say, "You?? School?? HA!HA!HA!"

Identify now anyone who may put you down for going to school for whatever reason. (Even if you don't complete any other exercise in this book, **PLEASE DO THIS ONE.**)

1)_____ 2)_____

3)_____ 4)_____

Now take a close look at the names you wrote down. If those people bring you down a lot, you need to ask yourself whether you would be better off without their brand of "friendship." If you're thinking you would feel bad about not being around them anymore, think about this: Why should you be heavy-hearted about spending less time with non-supporters? Wouldn't you support THEIR efforts to better themselves? Why shouldn't you have that type of support from them?

Listen, do not fall for king and queen hold-you-down-isms of all time from someone who is doing nothing may try to pull on you. For instance, you may hear, "Humph! Tryin' to sound White! Why do you talk like THAT!" I used to wonder why if you handled English well, you couldn't be Black. I wondered, that is, until I understood that that type of statement was just a king-size hold-me-down-ism **that I had the power to accept or ignore.**

What if a "friend" says to you, "You think you are better than I am because you are going to school!" The truth is THEY think you are better than they because **you are doing what they wish they had the courage to do.**

If you fall for hold-you-down-isms and, therefore, remain at their level, your "friends" will feel more comfortable WITH THEMSELVES because they KNOW they should be doing something more productive with their time. Now, if you'll notice, there's not a whole lot of thinking about YOU going on in their thinking. So, you will have to do your own thinking for and about yourself and your future. What advice kept Bernadette in school?

◆ Never take put-downs to heart. In fact, forgive the person putting you down simply because he or she speaks out of ignorance if the belief is held, for example, that one must belong to a particular race to handle English well — or that your attention towards education automatically turns you into a snob. You are not better than your friends just because you decided to continue your education — wiser certainly — not better.

◆ Set an example of success that your friends may want to follow. Share good grades, etc., but don't brag. They may be encouraged to go back to school but don't be self-righteous or haughty if they don't.

◆ Know that it is not at all unusual to move towards people who are doing the same thing as you are. Show yourself to be friendly in school and you'll soon find yourself not missing the old hang gang as much because new people will respond to your friendliness.

So stay on the path that leads to education and empowerment. Let others follow your lead. Just keep on going whether you are followed or not.

YOU CANNOT CONTROL HOW OTHERS BEHAVE OR WHAT THEY SAY, NOR SHOULD YOU BE CONTROLLED BY THEM. INFLUENCE OTHERS TOWARD THEIR HIGHEST GOOD, AND KEEP STEPPING TOWARD YOURS.

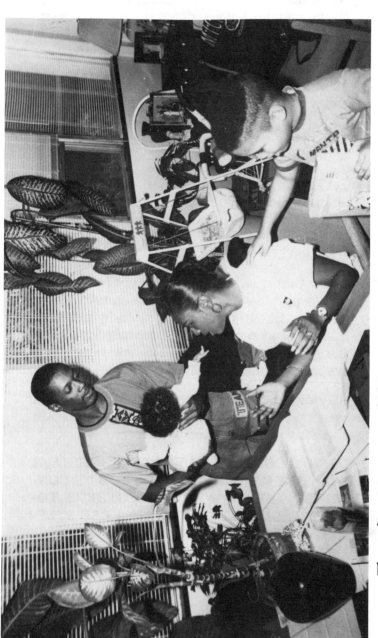

Those closest to you may bid for your attention to the point of distraction.

CHILD CARE

Rhonda's Story

A routine attendance check told me that Rhonda was on her third straight day of absence from her classes. I rang her up at home.

"Oh, hi, Ms. Lewis," she said cheerfully.

"Well you don't SOUND sick," I teased.

"Oh, I'm not sick," she said pleasantly.

"Oh. So...why have you been absent?"

"Nothing major. It's just that I don't have anyone to watch Corey. See, Melinda and I really got into it a couple of nights ago and...anyway, she sort of said she would never watch Corey again for me...and I don't have another sitter right now so..." she explained. Silence.

"So, Rhonda, what are you going to do?" I asked.

A pause. Then, "Do? About what?" she wondered.

"SCHOOL." I stated.

"Mrs. Lewis, I can't come if I don't have a sitter," she complained.

"My very point. You're getting behind in your classwork. Have you TRIED to get someone else?" I asked somewhat frustrated.

"Oh, that's not necessary," she said matter-of-factly. "Melinda will cool off. Trust me. I know my sister. And when we make up — and we always do — she will babysit again," she said confidently.

"But...but what about the work you're missing? What about the investment of tuition dollars you've made into yourself that you borrowed from the government?" I reminded her. A long pause. GOOD! I thought. I got through. Her reply?

"Mrs. Lewis, I can't come to school if I don't have a sitter." she continued.

Rhonda's sister didn't make up. Rhonda had to drop out.

To those of you who are parents: Unless you have a dependable that is, a steady, reliable, supportive-of-your-efforts babysitter — you will not be able to attend school regularly. And although most people arrange for a sitter before signing up for school, problems still occur if:

◆ The person you've asked to sit is careless or otherwise undependable.

◆ You enlist the services of family members or

friends and then permit arguments to destroy sitting arrangements.

◆ The sitter IS dependable but becomes seriously ill and you have no "emergency" sitter.

PROBLEM: You have an unreliable babysitter.

SOLUTION: Here are some general rules of thumb that will help you to clear this hurdle:

◆ Select a sitter from among people who WANT you to go to school. Your old hang gang buddy who is not in school, for example, may still enjoy hanging out during the week until 3 a.m. So it would be unreasonable for you to expect that person to be alert enough to watch your active preschooler in the mornings. Nor would he or she be willing to give up too many evenings in order for you to attend night classes.

◆ Be sure to make your sitter aware that he or she is not only responsible for your child's welfare in your absence, but plays a starring role in your success. You have to be in school in order to learn. You have to learn in order to graduate with any degree of marketable knowledge. It follows that **you very much need a dependable sitter in order to graduate.** Make a point of telling your sitter how important his or her services are to your success.

◆ RIGHT NOW — that is, BEFORE you are angry with each other — is the time for you to be in firm agreement with your sitter that neither of you will allow disagreements to disrupt child care and prevent you from graduating. Your sitter should agree to not "punish" you by withdrawing sitting services; and you should agree to not "punish" your sitter by stating in the heat of an argument about an unrelated matter that you no longer want him or her around your child. If the sitter is good enough to guard Junior for weeks at a time previous to an argument, then the sitter still has the same sitting talents AFTER the argument. Never allow your ego and pride to keep you from your cap and gown.

◆ Be absolutely clear about what you do and do not want your child exposed to in your absence. If, for instance, you don't allow harsh or x-rated language; strangers in the home; negative TV program selection; or spiritual doctrines contrary to your own being discussed with your child, SAY SO UP FRONT. You don't have to turn into a dictator or a self-righteous snob. Just explain without being judgmental what you do and don't want your child exposed to.

◆ Never take your sitter for granted. If your classes end at 3 p.m., but you don't get home until 6 p.m. everyday, expect your sitter to be upset if there was no agreement for you to be so late on a regular basis. And CALL if you have to stay at school to make up a test, etc. Your acts of common courtesy will help remind the sitter of how much you value his or her services.

In the spaces provided below, list people who are willing to help you conquer this potentially success-stopping hurdle:

_____ will sit for me while I'm in school.

_____ agrees to sit for me should the above-named person become unable to sit.

_____ and I agree that we will not permit any disagreement between us to cause me to lose his or her services unless it is a matter concerning the welfare of my child over which we disagree.

_____ will KNOW that I appreciate him/her because in addition to wages, I will show appreciation by

_____

_____

_____

That last point is very important. Be sure to give a little something extra to your sitter besides earned wages. A little extra appreciation in the form of a small gift or complimentary language can inspire your sitter to sit even if he or she feels a little under the weather.

There is peace of mind in knowing that your child is in good hands while you're away. You will need that reassurance in order to concentrate in your classes. If no one in your family or circle of friends is able to sit, try:

♦ A professional, LICENSED service;

♦ A reliable neighbor who may be willing to sit for extra income;

♦ Your school's bulletin board, or sitters other students use.

As always, be absolutely sure of the credentials of any person with whom you plan to leave your child. Investigate as many possibilities as possible. Know that your determination to find a quality sitter will be well paid in the form of peace of mind.

It is absolutely crucial that you arrange for reliable transportation.

TRANSPORTATION

Did you know that there are a remarkable number of students who, while caught up in the excitement of registering for school, forget they don't have a way to get to and from school regularly?

It's true. They borrow a family member's car to come in and sign up, but they've often made no provision for transportation beyond registration day.

It doesn't take a genius to figure out that if you can't attend, you will fall behind in your lessons. If you fall behind, you will want to throw up your hands in frustration and may want to quit. Obviously, then, this issue of transportation is not to be taken lightly. Ask yourself the following questions and then provide the answers:

1) How am I going to get to and from school daily?

_____

2) What is Plan B should Plan A fail?

_____

3) Are there people I can ask NOW, that is, BEFORE I need them, if they will help me see to it that I get to school one way or another? List them.

1)_____ 2)_____

3)_____ 4)_____

Now, since human beings are only human, chances are you still will need a few back-up plans. Therefore:

◆ Consider putting a few dollars away each week in a taxi jar just in case an emergency arises, such as your car breaks down on the day of a major exam.

◆ Learn the bus routes from home to school.

◆ Ask other students if they would be willing to car pool.

Please note this carefully: It is a common practice for employers to call a school and check students' records when they are considering hiring that school's grads. This is particularly true of business school grads. Among other questions, a favorite is, "What was his/her attendance record?" Please don't take this hurdle for granted. It is absolutely crucial that you arrange for reliable transportation.

PROFESSIONAL ATTIRE

Theodore's Story

"Mrs. Lewis," Theodore was saying patiently. "I fully understand your concern about my being able to fit into the mainstream, American work environment. However, I refuse to lose my individuality by dressing in a dark blue or black — or any other color — straight jacket for the rest of my working years. I can do my work well regardless of what I wear. If an employer is so superficial as to want to hire me based on how I look, well, I simply won't work there."

Theodore and I were going round for round about the school's dress code. The code requires students to dress "office ready" as much as their budgets would allow. Theodore not only didn't wear a suit and tie — or even a dress shirt and slacks — he wore sandals, khakis, an earring, and long hair. He had a 4.0 grade point average and was very well spoken. Unfortunately, he always looked as if he had just escaped from a refugee camp.

"...See, Mrs. Lewis," he was saying, "your problem — and it is common among many of you

21

post-sixties, now-the-establishment Blacks — is that you've been sucked into the system and are convinced that in order to get ahead, you have to all look alike."

"Theodore, you have a right to wear whatever you want," I said sincerely.

"Thank you." He got up to leave.

"And an employer feels he or she has a right to turn you down flat if you plan on dressing your own way for an interview," I continued.

He sat back down. "I already said I will not work for a company that hires based on appearance," he reiterated.

"Oh? Then you must be planning to open your own company," I challenged.

"Well... not right away. One doesn't rush into..." he responded cautiously.

"Then you will have to work for someone else," I stated.

"But NOT for a company that considers appearance as its main criteria in the selection process," he insisted.

"Then you'll be unemployed for a while because everywhere you apply, your appearance will be strongly taken into consideration," I warned.

"But that's not reasonable or fair," he insisted.

"But it IS fact. Fairness is not the issue. And

speaking of reasoning, the real question becomes, with your excellent grades, attributes, and communication skills, will you allow a golden opportunity to pass you by because you refuse to conform to a company's dress code? Or because you refuse to wear interview apparel?" I questioned.

"All right," he conceded. "IF it's for a position that's on my career path, and IF after researching the company I discover that it pays well, THEN I guess I'd consent to wearing the straight jacket. And that's ONLY for the interview, mind you. But once I'm hired..." he insisted again.

"Listen, Theodore, if you present yourself in any way differently AFTER you are hired from what you presented BEFORE you were hired, you will have willfully misrepresented yourself. That means you will have been hired under pretense. Your employer will resent having been tricked. You'll be dead, politically speaking. Do you really want to risk the chance of being promoted over this issue of dress?" I proposed.

"I hear you..." he said nodding.

Dear Reader: Will YOU be flexible enough in your attitude about your choice of dress in order to achieve goals that are far more important than having a "nonconformist's" wardrobe? If not, why not?

Let me share a story with you. Not too long ago, I bumped into one of my former graduates at a shopping mall. I almost didn't recognize her as I was used to seeing her wear enough rings, bracelets, chains, and earrings to open her own small boutique. She stood in front of me wearing only a few well-chosen pieces. After we chatted a moment, I remarked on how much more attractive she looked without her collection. I also teased her a little about the many verbal scrapes we used to have about her "right" to wear it. I admitted to being curious about what had caused the change. "I don't seem to need all of that any more," she said. What an honest response! She said she didn't NEED the jewelry any more. Those pieces had been her miniature shields. She had used them to hide her low self-esteem. She now was comfortable enough with herself that it was okay for others to see beyond her jewelry so she had removed the excess. Do you see yourself in this story? Do you hide behind jewelry, extra long nails, or unnatural hair colors or distracting hairstyles?

Maybe you are like many who believe that following a dress code means losing your individuality. Let's reason together:

◆ Individuality means existing as a person with qualities that set you apart from another person. What you wear can add to your individuality, or — as in the case of the excess jewelry wearer — can subtract from it. But, and this is the point, if you are really your own person, you could dress as an environment required and not lose sight of who you are as a person.

◆ Businesses require you to dress professionally. A professional is one who is engaged in an activity for the purpose of gain. So by demonstrating to an employer that you will dress for the job, you are signaling that you are willing to wear what is required for that business to appear gainful. You'll appear to be an employee who CARES. Caring employees are VALUABLE to employers.

- Business dressing is like putting on a costume. You should wear casual, "play" clothes when you are "playing" and business clothes when conducting business.

- A school's dress code is your chance to experiment with various colors, fabrics, and styles so that you can know which types of business costumes look best on you when it is time to interview in them.

What schools generally mean by "dress code" is that you're expected to look office ready regularly. You may be concerned enough to wonder what happens if you have to wear the same old clothes a couple of times a week. If the outfit is fresh, nothing. You will find plenty of other students wearing the same outfits often. If you find that there is a day or two in which you cannot comply with the dress code, DO NOT SKIP SCHOOL. You will quickly discover that your teachers would rather have you attend school in something that may be less than office ready than to have you miss your lessons.

Although problems in the area of dressing professionally can stem from financial considerations, problems also stem from a lack of resourcefulness. Many times, resourcefulness is choked by pride. Ask yourself whether you would consider using any of the following low- or no-cost options for building your professional wardrobe (and if you decide you wouldn't use any of these, why not? Are you allowing your pride to be a hold-you-down-ism?):

- Resale shops

- Rummage sales

- ◆ Clothes swapping

- ◆ Buying clothes out of season

- ◆ Bargain hunting at major department stores as well as lesser-known stores

- ◆ Losing weight in order to fit into "old" clothes

PROBLEM: You just went on an interview and left with the distinct impression that you are not going to get that job. Why, you ask yourself? You stop by to speak with your counselor and she asks, "Is that what you wore?"

SOLUTION: Companies and corporations all have a distinct image and impression that they want to give the people they service. You must be willing to adapt to the climate of the business that you wish to work in by dressing a certain way which not only reflects in the clothes you choose but also in the accessories as well, i.e.: shoes, jewelry, purses, hats, general neatness and cleanliness. Promptness is also crucial, so do attempt to be on time for that interview and after being hired.

Two major advantages to dressing professionally (notice I didn't say expensively) are:

- ◆ You will carry yourself with more confidence.

- ◆ Others will start to respond to you as if you SHOULD be respected.

Appearance is STILL within the top five reasons why people are or are not hired. Don't fight the dress code. See it as part of your professional development — a part of your training.

Your wardrobe can reflect your individuality but must be suitable for corporate America.

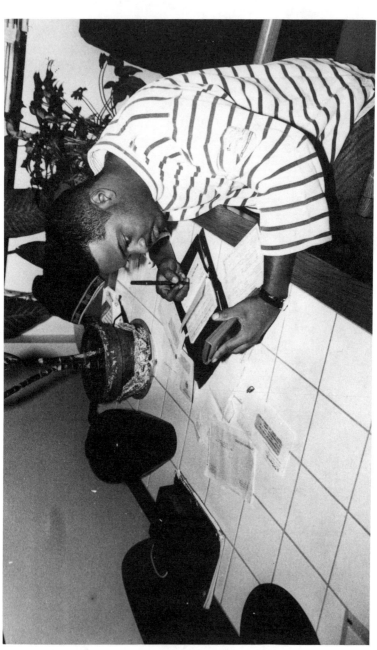

The most powerful tools you have to use for getting an education are your mind and your money, don't misuse either one.

HURDLE #5

FINANCIAL CONCERNS

Sally's Story

I caught up with Sally as she came out of her second class. "I need to see you," I said.

"Oh, yeah," she said. "I saw my name on the bulletin board but...uh..." She followed me to my office talking all the way. "I know what this is about, and I promise I'll catch up on my tuition..." We rounded a corner. "I had the money in my hand Mzz. Lewis. I swear it! I had it the day before yesterday. But there was this surprise party for my very best friend and..." We entered into my office, and I shut the door. "Well, you know how it is."

"Sally...," I began.

"Oh, Mrs. Lewis! It's so hard!" she blustered.

"Sally..." I tried to continue.

"Since I've been in school, I don't EVER have any spending money," she whined.

Sally was on general assistance and was a single parent of two. She had been awarded a

27

grant to help pay for school, and a local bank had given her a loan. Her out-of-pocket expense was only $30 per month. Yet, in the six months she'd been in school, she had not once made a payment on time. In fact, one month's payment ran into another's on more than one occasion.

"Sally," I said again as I took out a blank ledger sheet. "It's time to plan how you will pay back your loan..."

"My LOAN?" She looked frightened. "I... I thought... wait a minute. I only owe a tuition payment or two, right?"

"Yes, but if you stay on this path of financial crisis that you are on, you're not going to have the discipline it takes to pay back your loan. So we should begin now to..." I continued.

"Oh, I see," she said. "Excuse me, Mrs. Lewis, but, well, don't you think you're kind of dipping into my personal affairs here? I mean keeping me to the line about paying tuition is school business. But setting up a budget for me is...well, that's MY business." she complained.

"You are paying tuition so that I can help you develop personally. Anything that has to do with that development is my concern. Now you told me that after you brushed up on your typing and steno skills here, you were going to get a job and then go on to a university at night," I said, trying to get Sally to focus on her finances.

"That's my plan all right. But what has that to do with..." she whined.

"How are you going to pay for your university classes?" I inquired.

"Well, the new job will help and the rest will be with another loan. Probably through the same lender that is helping me for this program," she confidently responded.

"Probably. Unless, of course, you end up in default," I warned.

"Uh, what's that?" as she looked puzzled.

"That's what lending institutions say you are in when you don't pay back a loan on time," I explained.

"Oh, I'll pay them back," she responded.

"Not on the path you're on," I warned.

"What...what happens when you...default?" she wondered.

"Your plans start to crumble before your very eyes because you can't get another loan when you're in default from a previous one." Sally was eyeing the blank ledger sheet. "So, Sally, may I make your future plans for continuing your education also my business, please?" I asked.

Sally smiled sheepishly and nodded.

Get set to hear an ugly "B" word: BUDGET. You will need one if you're juggling bills for child care, tuition, transportation, rent or mortgage, food, miscellaneous expenditures, etc.

If you made a list of priorities (there's that all-important word again), and if investing in your future is near the very top of your list, take the time now to list everything you routinely spend money on. Your money wasters will surface. You'll know them when you see them. Eliminate them. It is interesting to note that we will budget if what we are making room for in our finances is important enough to us to sacrifice a few items. So, once again, it comes down to your asking yourself just how much are you willing to sacrifice for your own future. Are you spending too much money on any of the following?

◆ Cigarettes

◆ Video rentals

◆ Movie theatres

◆ Bar/lounge/nightclub/cabarets

◆ Snacks/junk food

◆ Video games

◆  (?)

You are not being asked to sit in the house for the rest of the time you are in training and do nothing for entertainment. In fact, and note this carefully, if you don't find constructive ways to relax, you run the risk of stressing out. If you learn how to handle the pressures of meeting school-related deadlines, you'll be able to transfer your stay-cool skills to work-related pressures. Therefore, learning how to relax is a NECESSARY part of your training. Running, swimming, biking, basketball, hiking, tennis, etc., cost little money if you don't fall into the gotta-have-the-right-clothes-for-each-activity trap.

Complete the exercise below to help determine if there is any money you now spend that could be better spent on items that contribute to your plans to stay on board the education train.

$ _____ for cigarettes x 30 days.

$ _____ for 6 video rentals per month.

$ _____ for 4 drinks at a lounge (etc) per month.

$ _____ for 10 fast food visits per month.

$ _____ for 2 CD's, cassettes, etc., per month.

$ _____ **TOTAL**

Add up all the figures you've listed. Is your total enough to pay a bill? To purchase an item of clothing that would help you to stay in compliance with a dress code? To have emergency cab fare in case your car breaks down? To purchase a gift for your sitter? List what you are willing to do without in order to finance your education.

1)_____ 2)_____

3)_____ 4)_____

PROBLEM: Your income is such that you cannot afford to go to school, you are depressed and you feel like your life is going nowhere.

SOLUTION: Realize that nothing will change if YOU

do not make the effort. There are financial aid programs that are available for low-income families and child care costs can be incorporated within your budget as well. These programs include grants, scholarships and loans that you can apply for through the government, private lending institutions and corporations. Make the librarian your friend. You can find useful resource material for financial aid at the library in addition to the financial advising available through your school.

REMEMBER: THE MOST POWERFUL TOOLS YOU HAVE TO USE FOR GETTING AN EDUCATION ARE YOUR MIND AND YOUR MONEY. DON'T MISUSE EITHER ONE.

INVEST IN YOURSELF. THE RETURN WILL BE PURE PROFIT.

The librarian and financial aid officer can be your best resources for grants, scholarships, and loans.

Good health, alertness, confidence, a sense of power and control are the benefits of a healthy diet.

HEALTH AND NUTRITION

I know. You have heard it all before. You already know about this health and nutrition stuff. For instance, you know that:

♦ You should eat a balanced diet of lean meats, vegetables, fruits, etc.

♦ The way to lose weight is to take in fewer calories and exercise more. Do the opposite to gain weight.

♦ Diet pills can be dangerous and should be used under the guidance of a physician.

♦ Sugar and salt should be used with moderation.

♦ Starving yourself all day and then gorging on one meal—especially at bedtime—makes a very sluggish digestive tract and contributes to weight gain.

Even if you have heard it all before, resist the temptation to skip this section. There may be something you've forgotten or didn't know. For instance:

♦ You do not have to eat fried food — or any other heart-stopping fatty food lovingly referred to as "soul food" in order to make the family cook feel good. Those foods, although good to the taste buds, are evil regulators for your blood pressure, heart, and digestive tract.

◆ Marijuana is NOT safe and is an effective **memory ERASER.**

◆ You CAN become addicted to caffeine whether you take it from coffee, tea, pop, or chocolate.

◆ It is absolutely an act of suicide to breathe in carbon monoxide, a lethal poison. Yet some do this daily by smoking cigarettes. **(Note:** Offices are becoming smokeless because of sensitive equipment, better employee attendance from non-smokers, and fewer health risks which reduce insurance costs.)

Imagine a mobile, self-starting, highly efficient, well-constructed engine. You know that engines require gas and lubricants. You also know that if a manual says to put in a high grade of what that engine needs in order for it to run its best and you consistently put in a low grade, you should not expect that engine to run its best.

You're like an engine; the engine that houses the most advanced computer in the world — your brain. What does **your** "manual" say about you? If, for instance, you are prone to high blood pressure, or your cholesterol level is too high and you are running the risk of breaking down by means of a stroke, do you still feed on stroke-producing foods? If hot, spicy foods put gaseous bubbles in your digestive tract, do you eat those foods anyway because your tongue enjoys the taste? Do you eat gooey, but beautifully decorated, desserts — knowing that you will suffer later — just because your eyes and taste buds wanted you to eat those desserts?

If only your eyes and your tongue determine what you eat, you are more likely to select foods that weaken your entire system in the long run. Don't sacrifice the health of your entire system by eating foods selected by your eyes and tongue.

A word about "lubricants": Water your system. Don't alcohol it as a substitute, or Kool-Aid it, or coffee/tea/Coke it. WATER it. Try this experiment for ten days: Drink six to eight glasses of water (not all at once) each day and don't eat fried, salty, or sugary foods during that time. The results may not be seen on the scale (unless you eat less and exercise more), but you will notice a beautiful change in your complexion. That alone is worth trying the experiment.

Here are a few more reminders:

♦ Beware of low fat/no fat foods. Not all are safe if taken in large quantities. Check with a physician.

♦ Be aware of exactly what you are putting in your body. That means you will have to take that extra few seconds to read labels on packages and containers. I'll bet you didn't know that a well-known brand uses beef fat in its cupcakes.

♦ Take your blood pressure medication as prescribed by your doctor. Have your cholesterol level checked regularly.

Since a sluggish, ill-fed, over or underweight body will serve you poorly as you try to comprehend your school lessons, you must maintain a healthy weight. Answer yes or no to this short quiz:

♦ Do you think you are too fat or too skinny? _____

◆ When people want to make fun of you, do they pick on your weight? _____

◆ Do you find yourself sneaking a look at the waistlines of others and wishing you could look the way they do? _____

◆ When you stand or sit, do you find yourself holding packages, books, or whatever you happen to be carrying over your midsection because you are uncomfortable about your fat or thinness? _____

If you answered yes to ANY of the above, take a long look at yourself in a full-length mirror — being certain to check all angles of yourself. If you see there is room for improvement, get started on your campaign for positive change now. The benefits include:

◆ Alertness in your classes and an ability to grasp your lessons more quickly.

◆ More confidence in yourself and more pride in your appearance.

◆ A sense of power and control over your own being.

One of the most important factors that is often overlooked or neglected is getting the proper amount of rest. Without getting the right amount of sleep, you cannot function very well —whether it be with your children, in class or at work. A tired body can cause you to be short tempered, irritable with others, careless and forgetful. Make sure you get the proper amount of sleep so that you can do well on those "all-important exams" and so that once you land that job you can perform up to par and don't find yourself falling behind because you are sluggish. Make the effort to schedule your time so that you are alert when you need to be. Remember that appearance IS CRUCIAL. Interviewers WILL turn you down if you seem careless about your appearance. And this applies **NO MATTER HOW SHARP YOUR SKILLS MAY BE.** Understand that an employer seeks to hire a PACKAGE. A company does not seek just your fast fingers for typing, shorthand, computing, etc. Each scrutinizes the ENTIRE package. So don't wait until you graduate to start your shape-up campaign. Get a running start now — while you're still in training.

ATTENDANCE

Hilda's Story

"Wait, let me get this straight," Hilda said to me in disbelief. "You're saying that by signing this...this... probation paper, I'm AGREEING that you can put me out of here if I continue to take days off?" she said incredulously.

"Hilda, the term is only three weeks old and you've already missed five days — that's ONE THIRD of your training up to this point. Now, I have been giving you warnings all along. So now for your own good..." I firmly said.

"Listen," she said hotly. "I am paying to go to school out of my own pocket. I come when I feel I can come. It's MY money," she insisted.

"Yes, it is. And you're making a purchase with your money, right?" I continued.

"Well...yes...in a way I suppose..." she responded defensively.

"Yes. You're purchasing a training program. Now don't you want to take what you're buying home with you — that is, in your brain — and then on with you to your future place of employment?" I suggested.

Silence. Thinking.

"Then you simply have got to come to school," I emphasized. I placed a pen on top of the probation form and slid the paper towards her. "Yes, Hilda, it is your money. That's why this probation is not punishment. It is a training tool. You are paying to learn how to please an employer. Dropping in and out at your own leisure as if the place were a Holiday Inn is not how it's done," I explained. It took her a moment, but she finally reached for the pen.

A major part of your training at any school is your own personal development in the form of a sense of responsibility. Even with your attendance record, you are preparing for employment. This means you must, among other things, notify your teachers (your bosses) whenever you are unable to report to classes (duty). You would be expected to call in if you were employed. See, employers believe that if you neglected to attend something you paid for, you would be just as likely — if not more so— to skip (work) if THEY were paying (in the form of a paycheck). Sounds reasonable.

Set good habits now. It is poor self management to allow your attendance record to show columns of no call/no show. There are many employers who would consider you to have abandoned your position if you are off a couple of days and have not called in. You would be subject to dismissal. Know your school's attendance policy, and follow it.

NOTE: If you are involved in legal proceedings that you expect will prevent you from attending your classes, please make your instructors aware of your obligations BEFORE you have to go. If you are served notice to report for jury duty or are served with a subpoena, etc., make a school official aware ahead of time of the date(s) you expect to be out. Please **do not just disappear.** Why risk being placed on attendance probation or being dismissed? Speak up about impending legal proceedings. You don't have to reveal personal details. You do, however, need to give dates you expect to be out and a general reason.

Food for thought: Employers, loan officers, etc. ROUTINELY call schools to ask about students':

◆ Attendance

◆ General attitude

◆ Grade point averages

◆ Programs or subjects studied.

Notice what is listed first. Guard your attendance record. Keep it clean. Demonstrate your sense of responsibility by calling in if you have to be out and by asking your teachers for a list of assignments or tests missed. You would be surprised at the number of students who miss tests and end up with low overall scores because they never asked what was covered while they were out.

Did you know that even if you have a history of poor attendance at former jobs prior to attending school, an employer will give a great deal of weight to your most recent attendance record? That would be your school record. Think about that. Your school record is your shot at starting afresh. Don't blow it.

WHY PAY TO GO TO SCHOOL AND THEN NOT GO?

All of the other hurdles tie directly into attendance. You can easily see why you can't take any of the hurdles for granted. Remember: CAREFUL PLANNING is the key to success.

CONCLUSION

Education is not something to be dismissed because there are foreseeable or unforeseeable circumstances that may prevent you from considering that endeavor.

I have attempted to present in a straightforward manner some of the major hurdles that you may encounter in trying to achieve your dreams of a better future and life for your family. These hurdles can be summarized briefly as being those within yourself, namely your attitude, self-esteem, lack of confidence and discipline and those outside yourself: those family members, friends and circumstances such as transportation, health, child care problems and negative feedback from potential employers that may prevent you from attaining your goal.

All of us want a better life for ourselves but few of us attain the satisfaction of reaching out for our dreams and making those dreams a reality. When you ask yourself those questions late in the evening hours and are plagued by worries, bills, and problems, are you content with the money that you receive and the respect that you get from your friends, neighbors, family and people in your community or would you like to strive for something more?

That something more may take several years to attain but it all begins with one step. That step can begin with this book — a handbook to help you understand what lies ahead on that path and to help you form an effective PLAN before you get into trouble and find yourself wondering how you got into such a mess and what to do next BEFORE dropping out becomes a reality.

One of the problems with the African American community is that we have so much talent and ability but have not effectively CHANNELED our energies in the right directions. Being an effective role model for your children and setting an example for them to follow, an inspiration, and someone for them to strive to walk in their footsteps should not be a matter taken lightly. So, when you plan your future, plan it wisely.

Being poor has its problems, but not utilizing the talent and ability that you were born with is a crime to yourself and the people that you could be helping. Why not take the time to do the exercises outlined in this book and think about what you can do to make your life better for yourself and your loved ones as well as effectively impact your environment.

As you read through this handbook, you found examples of situations that you may encounter during school, the interview process as well as employment selection guidelines. Reread the recommendations on attendance and professional attire as you plan to step into the professional work force and develop into the person you can be.

You need not settle for less than what you can become. The greatest failure is not attempting to try. Seek out the assistance of the counselors that your school has provided and don't be afraid to ask questions of your instructors —even those you consider to be "stupid". Others have made it before you and despite the odds, i.e.: lack of financial assistance, no time to study, etc. If you make the effort, you will find that others will assist you once you make up your mind, with firm determination that no matter what, you will finish.

After you have finished and have gotten that all-important "job" and can smile at the days you thought you just couldn't make it, just remember that the careful planning that it took to bring you to that point, the skills you acquired and your discipline are transferable to any endeavor you undertake in life.

The criteria used to evaluate a professional as well as how you conduct your life determines the level of success you will achieve not only in school but throughout your relations with others in your community, your work environment, and your home.